The Forgiveness Process

Ann Thomson

A catalogue record for this title is available from the British Library.

ISBN 0-9552625-0-X

(ISBN 978-0-9552625-0-0)

Printed and bound in the UK by Antony Rowe Ltd., Bumpers Farm Industrial Estate, Chippenham, Wilts.

Published by Purgl Publishing,
            The Paddock,
            Mount Pleasant,
            Newburgh,
            Fife, Scotland.
            KY14 6AD

Contents

Introduction

This book may never have been written but for the encouragement of the holistic physician who treated my illness so successfully. He convinced me that my thoughts on forgiveness would, in varying measure, be meaningful to others. The total belief of my family in my ability to complete the project enabled me to persevere. I accepted and completed the challenge. Thank you to those who helped me to see it through to the end.

When I began my search for a solution to the problem of unforgiveness I could never have foreseen the way it would change my life so completely. As an organised individual, it appeared logical to me to slowly and meticulously work in a systematic fashion throughout the events of my life. The "Forgiveness Process" evolved. This process worked for me. As I put my theories into practice, my self-awareness became more acute and I began to see the multiplicity of reasons why human beings act the way they do.

This is not a quick fix method. It is a process of change. It is about dealing with past and present hurts and traumas. It is about becoming the finer person you were meant to be. It is a way of life. It is a way to become a forgiving person, a human being at peace with the world and themselves.

"When we hate our enemies, we give them power over us – power over our sleep, our blood pressure, our health and our happiness. Our enemies would dance for joy if they surmised that they worry and lacerate us. Our hatred is not hurting them at all; it only turns our own days and nights into hellish turmoil."

Author Unknown

"Resentment is like taking poison, yet expecting the other person to die."

Author Unknown

Chapter 1

Why Forgive?

The Background

Early one autumn morning I awoke to the nightmare of an extreme vertigo attack. The room whirled around relentlessly as I clung to either side of the mattress convinced that I was going to be sucked into the swirling mass of horror that faced me each time I opened my eyes. Nothing was solid in my world. Everything in the room had turned into one gigantic whirlpool which rotated so fast that I felt that I would be drawn in and become part of it. As I clung, fingers like claws, to the only thing that offered any measure of comfort and screamed for my husband, my whole Being felt terrified. He arrived after what seemed an endless time and was totally shocked at my condition. I had been suffering from vertigo attacks for about four years, and had been medically retired early from teaching, but this was the most severe attack to date. I could not move for an endless time. I finally let go of the mattress when the picture in front of my eyes gradually returned to normal. Even then I could not move my head from side to side, even a fraction, without the extreme symptoms returning.

A locum G.P. made a house call but could only offer higher doses of prescription medicine, which was sedative in nature. Although she was very sympathetic, she told me there was nothing more that could be done to help me.

For the next three days I was completely dependent on my husband to wash and feed me. I could not stand. I could not sit up without piles of pillows to support me. He even had to help me to the toilet. I had absolutely no sense of balance. Gradually over the days that followed I began to regain some control. The first day that I stood up without keeling over seemed like a miracle. It took another month before I felt that I could venture out of doors and, even then, I was so afraid that I would fall and hurt myself. My confidence had been badly knocked and I wondered if I would ever have the courage to go out alone again.

Eventually I did. The urge to remain at home, where I knew I was safe was extremely strong, but I forced myself to go out. I knew that it was essential to build up my confidence if I was to survive and live an independent life.

Depression was the other giant that needed to be slain. My confidence had been battered. I felt and looked so ill all the time. I was exhausted and had been told that there was no cure for my medical condition. In fact I really did not know if or when the horror would start again. The thought of living with that knowledge for the rest of my life was not appealing.

At the onset of my illness I had been diagnosed as having Benign Paroxysmal Positional Vertigo. This means that certain head movements could trigger vertigo attacks of varying intensity at any time. The condition affected my balance to varying degrees and caused severe neck pain and headaches. I had been prescribed medication to ease these symptoms but it had obviously done nothing to prevent the attacks. I was taking tablets for vertigo, pain relief and for another, perhaps related problem, insomnia. All of these tablets had a sedative affect; dulling my senses and making me feel lethargic

Excellent treatment at my local hospital had done little to alleviate my condition. I had x-rays to my neck, which showed loss of curvature. I had an M.R.I. scan of my head to check for tumours. Thankfully there were none. At this point I was given a collar to wear for a short time each day and told I would be seen in six months. I felt abandoned. I felt alone with a condition which, although not life threatening, was very distressing and very frightening. I just never knew when the next attack would be, when I would next fall over or how I would feel from day to day.

Luckily I managed to get a referral to the physiotherapy department where I was given heat treatment and acupuncture, which helped the neck pain and headaches. Unfortunately it did nothing for the vertigo symptoms. I was then transferred to the neurology department where the consultant told me that my problem was so acute because I had two separate conditions, loss of neck curvature and damage to the inner ear. Lack of curvature meant that the blood supply to my brain was restricted when I moved my head in certain directions causing me to be extremely dizzy or, at times, suddenly fall to the ground. Damage to the inner ear caused the continual, extreme vertigo attacks and loss of balance. It was my bad luck to have both. Further physiotherapy was arranged within this department.

A programme of exercises design to re-educate the brain to accept head movements was started with a very patient and caring therapist. These were called Cooksey-Cawthorne exercises and need to be practised at least four times daily. At first I could only move my head very slightly before the attacks began but, with persistence and encouragement, I began to make progress. (She told me that I was the worst case of vertigo she had seen.) I was asked to reduce my medication if possible to make the exercises more effective. I managed to halve the dosage but could not cope on less. Over a period of six months I managed to complete the programme. At the end I was told that I should be O.K. as long as I was not over tired or unwell with something else.

This proved to be the case and I survived reasonably well for about two years as long as I was very, very careful. I was still unable to work, take part in sport, dance, cope confidently with housework or do supermarket shopping but at least I felt less fearful. The attack described at the beginning of this chapter came after a week of feeling extremely tired. It was the most severe since the initial ear infection, which caused all these symptoms.

My husband knew that I was at my lowest ebb. I was so ill, so low, and so reluctant to face a life punctuated with continual attacks, which seemed to be getting worse instead of better. There was also a myriad of other symptoms to cope with daily (see Appendix A), which made life so restrictive. I just looked into the future and saw a life of illness. The bright, positive, able person, that I used to be, seemed to have disappeared.

Luckily my husband had heard of a holistic physician from an associate who, he was convinced, could help me and persuaded me to make an appointment. Choosing to do this would prove to be one of the most important decisions of my life. It gave me the opportunity to find my way back to wellness i.e. good health, confidence, positive outlook, happiness and feeling glad to be alive.

This appointment was made about two months after the extreme attack previously described. After extensive diagnostic testing, he told me, among many other things, that I had an overwhelming need to forgive. I agreed that this was true but also stated that for most of my life I had been a very forgiving person. This had gradually changed over the years as I felt more and more "put upon" by the people I came in contact with. I began to feel angry and resentful, gradually and unwittingly building up a mountain of unforgiveness. I realise now that I did not truly know how to forgive but I was to find out over the next few months.

I returned home that day wondering how I was to proceed. I had been given no guidelines but I knew that learning to forgive was crucial to my regaining good health. I was absolutely determined to find an answer to my problem. The following chapters outline the discoveries that I made. I hope they are meaningful to you.

*"You cannot run away from a weakness; you must
sometime fight it or perish and if that be so,
why not now, and where you stand."*

Robert Louis Stevenson

Chapter 2

Forgive them for they know not
what they do!
Luke 23:34

For most of my life I thought that I had been a reasonably forgiving person. I had attended church faithfully since childhood, had been a Sunday school teacher, been married in church and had my children baptised in church. I had prayed and read my bible regularly but had obviously missed the true concept of forgiveness. The reason I tell you all these things is to show you that a person can do all the supposed "right" things and yet still be so far from a true understanding. I thought that forgiveness was for the comfort of the other people in the situation. I did not realise that it was for my welfare too. I had stopped letting them "off the hook" by my way of thinking and had unwittingly damaged myself. I was to discover that forgiveness is a wonderful way to freedom of spirit and freedom to be yourself. It is the way God meant us to be.

I had been told that I had an enormous need to forgive and I accepted that this was true. I had tried so many times to sort out my life but somehow could not let go of the things from the past that tormented me. I think it was because I kept asking "Why?" Why had people said or done certain things, when I thought I had done nothing to deserve it?

I tried to look at my life as an examiner, an observer, so that I could be as objective as possible. I decided that it did not matter why. The important thing was, not the reasons why, but the state of my health. A plan was needed. To ensure that I missed nothing I chose to review the whole of my life in meticulous detail. If forgiveness was the key to better health I was determined to do as thorough a job as possible. I had nothing to lose and everything to gain. I had been told that there was nothing further that my GP could do to help my condition so this was a possible way forward. It was a ray of hope in a very bleak landscape.

To ensure that I did not miss anything that might delay the healing process I decided to think over the whole of my life from early childhood to the present day. To achieve maximum effect, I reviewed easily recognised areas of development e.g. early childhood, school days, further education, working life, marriage, having children etc. in sequential order. (See examples at the end of the chapter.) Working in each of these time blocks took several days, sometimes a whole week, since I had to think deeply over each area, pinpointing as much detail as possible, however insignificant it might seem. Some areas took longer than others. Often it was very painful and upsetting and many tears were shed.

As I remembered incidents and the people involved, I tried to be as rational and as objective as I could so as not to colour the process with emotion. I tried to remember everyone present, not just the main characters. Often we only recall the stinging look or the hurtful words and forget the context. It is important to see the whole picture. I tried to see everything in my mind's eye. I thought about clothing, hair, body language, situation, who was present and what everyone said or did. I began to realise that there were possible reasons why people had acted in certain ways, to see the big picture instead of the tiny part that had hurt me. Often I could see where I had unwittingly contributed to problems. Since I could see this, I was able then to forgive more easily. I could forgive the ones who had hurt me and forgive myself too. If I could not see a reasonable explanation I still forgave. I told myself that it happened a long time ago, it was making me ill and it was time to let it go. The other people concerned had probably never thought about it again or had been totally unaware that any offence had occurred. They were happily getting on with their own life and it was time I did the same.

As I finished each block, I talked it over with my husband. Most of the time he just listened, which is what I needed him to do, but we did discuss areas of common ground, which lead to further enlightenment. By talking it over with him, I started to understand the wider implications. I then said aloud to him that I totally forgave all the people and situations. It was enormously healing to say it out loud. I said "I forgive you", opened my arms out wide and said "and I let it all go!" The joy of release was wonderful.

It is important to open your arms to let go. You may think this somewhat theatrical but think about I like this. When you are upset, stressed, angry or resentful you may frequently sit with arms or legs crossed or both. This increases tension on your body. It's as if you are holding on tightly to all the hurts and refusing to let go. Do you really want to do that? When you have gone through the forgiveness process, when your heart tells you to let go, open your arms wide and say it aloud.

Say: "I forgive you and I let it all go!"

This affirmation is very important. It is important to speak aloud. Don't just whisper. Speak in a very positive, loud voice. Tell yourself and anyone else that you want to hear. Say it and mean what you say!

I continued doing this with each block in turn. This first part of the process took me about a month working on it every day. It may take you a longer or shorter time. Remember that this is a very personal adventure. Take all the time you need but don't dwell on incidents too much. When I went back to see the holistic physician at the end of that month, he was astonished with the results of the tests he did that day. **The overpowering need to forgive was gone.** I was not completely free but the enormous burden had disappeared. This was only the beginning. I have continued to explore forgiveness. It is a daily part of my life. It continues to cleanse me and set me free. It is an ongoing adventure.

Suggested blocks to cover the Forgiveness Programme

In each block think about home, family, friends, teachers, school, boyfriends, girlfriends, spouse, own children, in-laws etc.

1. **Childhood up to going to school**
   Feeling unloved
   Sibling rivalry

2. **Primary school years**
   Being chastised by teacher
   Bullying
   Family problems
   Financial restrictions
   Broken friendships

3. **Secondary school years**
   Cultural differences
   Emotional hurts
   Problems understanding the nature of relationships
   Sexual ignorance

4. **Further education**
   Living away from home
   Opinions of other students
   Differences in upbringing

5. **Starting first job**
   Problems fitting in
   Difficulties with boss

Bullying
Stress

6. **Meeting future partner**
Differences of opinions
Life values
Moral standards
Religion

7. **Partners family**
Parental control
Sibling rivalry
Cultural differences

8. **Marriage**
Financial worries
Partners working hours
Life goals

9. **Children**
Personality
Medical problems
Education

10. **Yourself**
This is the hardest bit to do.
In order to forgive myself I had to:-

- Accept the mistakes of the past.

- Accept that I am a human being and human frailty is part of life.

- Accept, without regret, all my missed opportunities. (I did make a promise to myself not to miss any more.)

- Accept that decisions made in the past were made in the light of the experience, circumstances and knowledge I had at that time.

"The journey of a thousand miles begins with one step."

Lao-tse

15

Chapter 3

The Forgiveness Process Stage 1

Initial Trawling Over Life from Childhood to Present

1. **Think over the whole of your life to ensure that you do not miss anything that will delay the healing process. Start as far back as you can remember and move through the months and years trying to recall all the events that have disturbed you in any way. Do not miss anything out, however insignificant it may appear. If you feel even the slightest twinge of resentment, anger, huffiness, sadness, grief etc. the incident needs to be dealt with. Do this in manageable blocks. (See pages 12-14)**

2. **Decide not to ask the reasons why events happened. The important issue is gaining good health and happiness in your life, not going over the "Why's" and apportioning blame.**

8. **Make a quiet time each day to work on forgiveness. Go and sit by yourself where you will not be disturbed. If you have other people that share your home ask them not to disturb you.**

4. **Close your eyes and reach back as far as you can into your memories and allow events to flow into your mind.**

5. **As you remember incidents and the people involved try to be as rational as you can in your thinking. Try not to**

colour the process with emotions. Remember that many of the things will have happened when you were a child, teenager or young adult and your reactions when remembering would usually be governed by your response at that age. Try to use the experience of the years to take a more adult view.

6. Look at the whole picture in your mind's eye as if you are an observer watching an action replay. Be objective. Look at everyone in the scene. Look at their faces, body language, the interaction and the part you played in it all. Look at the situation each event took place in. Examine the scene. You may see people and actions that you had not focused on before. You will begin to see possible reasons for the parts everyone had to play and with this will come some measure of understanding.

7. You may see the possible reasons why the people involved acted or spoke the way they did. You then begin to see the "Big Picture" not just the little bit that affected you.

8. Even if you can't understand tell yourself:-

- that it was a long time ago.
- that the other people concerned had probably never thought about it again.
- that they may have been totally unaware that they had ever caused any offence or hurt.
- that you may be punishing yourself again and again over something that happened when you had no control over the events.

- that you did not have enough life experience or expertise to make wiser choices.

9. As you finish each block talk it over, if possible, with a close relation or friend, someone you can trust with your deepest hurts. If you would rather not do this go to a quiet place and say it aloud. The act of voicing your deepest hurts is important. It is enormously healing. You will begin to see the wider implications.

10. Once you have talked through an area say aloud,
      "I forgive you and I let it all go".

11. Do this with each block in turn.

12. Be absolutely meticulous. Don't be tempted to miss bits out thinking that you can speed the process up. If you want to be well, if you want to be happy you must clean out all the debris.

13. Now use the same process to review the *good things* in your life. This is very important since it gives a balanced view and finishes the process on a brighter, happier, more positive note. People who have a great need to forgive are frequently tense, overworked, depressed, ill individuals who have lost the ability to see the good in situations. Therefore, work just as hard at reviewing the happy, successful times to balance the forgiveness process. Both are important to your feelings of well being. At the end of this stage hug yourself (hold on to these memories) and say thank you for all your blessings, opportunities, and happiness.

"The most difficult thing in life is to know yourself"

Thales

Chapter 4

Onward and Upward

As your ability to forgive grows you will become a different kind of person. Everyone has the ability to become, to change, to develop, to grow into a more patient, more tolerant, more confident individual. Learning to forgive helps you do this. It helps you to manage the hurts that life throws at you. It does not make them disappear. Life isn't like that. Since life is a continual learning process and the problems we face are the learning blocks, we must find ways to solve the problems we meet effectively. Forgiveness gives us the tools to do this. It teaches us to stand back, look at the whole picture, examine the issues and reach solutions.

 As soon as you have finished Stage 1 you must begin to implement changes in the way you conduct your life and in the way you think. Once the negatives have been dealt with you will have "thinking" space that has been vacated by the cleansing. This must be filled by positive action, otherwise old thinking habits may return. Changes need to be made. Here are some indications of the way forward.

1. <u>Learn to say "No"</u>

Learn to say "No" nicely. Many disputes are about control although most people would neither recognise this nor admit it. The two extremes in this area are the person who says "Yes" too often and the opposite type who says "No". If you are a "Yes" person you will find yourself agreeing to do things that you really don't want to do and feeling resentful afterwards. Others may think you are wonderful since you are always available to:-

- run errands
- baby-sit
- do extra work
- take over at the last minute
- lend money

or they think you are a wimp who can be taken advantage of. People may know you do not have the confidence to refuse and ask you to accommodate them, knowing full well that the request will put you under pressure.

If you are a "No" person you may feel that you should think about everything in detail before making a decision or you may lack in self-confidence. This will make you refuse:–

- invitations to social events
- career opportunities,
- offers of practical help
- demonstrations of affection
- advice from family and friends

This will inevitably lead to feelings of being left out, marginalized, isolated, lonely, unloved etc. You may become resentful and blame others for the situation you are in; after all it must be someone else's fault. It couldn't possibly yours.

However you will need to learn various ways of saying "No" since a blunt refusal may cause offence. You could respond by saying something like:-

- "I would rather not at the moment".
- "I don't have the time do that right now".
- "I have made another arrangement for that day/time".
- "I'd rather not lend you money any more".
- "I'm not comfortable with this situation".

Somewhere in between the two is a more balanced place to be. Both types of people need to learn this. Think before you make a decision. If you are unsure ask for, or simply take the time to think about it always remembering that you can't have everything your own way. Compromise is often the best way forward unless the matter is clear-cut.

However if all your instincts shout a loud "No", if you strongly disagree don't do it e.g., Next time your best friend asks you to lend them anything say "No" firmly and really mean it. Don't look guilty. Speak confidently and stick to what you say.

The opposite also applies. If everything in you screams a "Yes" response, do it. You may feel that you don't have the skills or the confidence to do it, however skills can be acquired and confidence grows when you learn to make firm decisions.

Make your "No" and your "Yes" quite clear to yourself and to everyone else. You do not need to be angry or aggressive to do this. State your case clearly, firmly and calmly. You have a right to be heard. This takes practice but like every new learning process it does become easier.

2. Be Aware of How You Conduct Yourself

Get into the habit of being the kind of person that *you* want to be regardless of how the other people in your life behave. Frequently we allow the way we behave to be dictated by other people. We get caught up in repeated behaviour patterns going over the same ground again and again. We react to their words and actions allowing them in effect to control our lives.

Think about the kind of person you want to be and do what you need to do to make it happen. You may need to change certain things in your life. Visualize the kind of person you would like to be. Hold onto that picture and work on the areas that you will need to alter developing the image and qualities that you would like to have.
You may have to change :–

- the language you use
- the tone of your voice
- the way you look at people
- your attitude to others
- your behaviour
- the way you dress
- your daily hygiene
- the food you eat
- your education programme
- your occupation

This will, of course, take some time, but gradually the change will occur. There will be times when you will slip back into old routines, think in the old negative ways and allow people to upset you.

Each time this occurs, take a mental note to stop yourself as soon as it happens. Note the things that trigger it so that you build up an awareness of the danger signs. Walk away, if necessary. Change what you are doing. Don't give up. It is not easy but it is the way forward.

There is no point in saying that you want things to be different and doing nothing to make it happen. Most people think that life would improve if only other people were different. Everything would be the way they wanted it to be if everyone else ironed out their faults or changed in certain ways. There is no point in wanting other people to be different and remaining the same yourself. You must be prepared to make changes. If you change you will find that those around you may change too. But, don't wait for others to give you permission to live. Act! Do something now! Be the person you have always wanted to be and do what you need to do to make it happen.

3. **Communication**

Poor communication causes a myriad of problems. Make a point of voicing your thoughts clearly and precisely so that you are completely understood. State clearly what you want and what you think. Don't be afraid of what others might think or say. You have a right to be heard therefore be prepared to stand on what you say and do. Effective communication is vitally important
This does not, however, give you the right to be hurtful or offensive in any way. Choose what you say carefully, taking care to think of the words you use and the tone of your voice. Stop thinking that you always have to "have your say" on

24

everything. Of course you will have your own opinions but you don't necessarily need to voice them all the time. Some things are best left unsaid or reserved for a more appropriate time. Once a hurtful word is spoken it cannot be taken back. Be careful what comes out of the mouth! Your words are the reflection of your thoughts.

4. **Boundaries**

Many situations get out of control because no boundaries are set. People within family groups should set boundaries of acceptable behaviour, rules for living that everyone knows and generally agree to. Without boundaries chaos reigns since no one has the security of guidelines for living. Resentment, anger, jealousy and stress can build up leading to high levels of unforgiveness and eventually poor health.

If no one else in your family group wants to deal with this area, do it yourself. Set your own boundaries and standards. Make up your mind what you are prepared to accept and live within your own boundaries. Don't allow others to cross or move them. This is where your "Yes" and "No" become firmer. Decide what is comfortable for you and only negotiate within your own limits.

5. **They Do Because They Can**

People only do and say things because they can, because others either do not have the courage to challenge them or don't even realise that it is possible to do something about it. If we allow the people in our lives to conduct themselves in a way that they come to think is acceptable, they will continue to do so unless challenged or ignored. Then they might say things like:-

- "I've always done that."
- "You didn't say anything before."
- "You're supposed to…"
- "You must…"
- "Everyone does this".
- "It's the way I am".

and a whole host of other reasons to keep life the way they want it to be. Your challenge is to be brave enough to ask for change and to insist that it takes place. Changes need to be planned and then implemented. They do not just happen. Think of where you are right now and where you want to go. Now separate the desired change pattern into easily achievable steps. Work on each step until successful before trying the next one. Each stage may take some time. Keep going since the alternative is going back to scratch. Is this what you really want to do?

When going through this process I say to myself: "Do you really want to go down that same old road again?" The answer is always "No". Although change is difficult I would rather go forward than repeat the mistakes of the past. The only way to develop the personality is to change, to develop new ideas, to develop new behaviour patterns and to accept opportunities as they present themselves.

6. Think for Yourself

Listen to and consider other peoples' opinions but think about how, and if, they apply to you. Sift through information and only use what you consider is relevant. In other words, think for yourself. Don't be continually swayed by the thoughts, ideas and opinions of others.

7. Acceptance

Life will never be perfect. The people in your life will never be perfect and neither will you. It is not possible. Trying to make it so only leads to heartache and confusion. Try to be kind to yourself when situations do not work out.
Perhaps life is trying to tell you something like:-

- Try again.
- Try something different.
- Try another way
- This is not for you

Some situations have to be accepted since no solution is apparent at that time. This does not mean that they will never change. Perhaps a remedial programme of small changes needs to be put into action before a conclusion is reached. Some problems are never going to be resolved. These you either accept and move on, walk away from or ignore.
Some things cannot be changed at the present time. Think about the timing of events in your life and sort into:–

- What can be done now?

- What can be done in the near future?
- What needs to be left on hold till an appropriate time?
- What cannot be changed and must, therefore, be accepted?

8. Recognise What Is Real

Often we have ideas of how we think life *should* be, how people *should* act, how happy we *should* be, how we *should* be treated etc. Sort out what is real in your life. Differentiate between what is fact and what is not. Your life may not be the way you would like it to be but you must start to change by dealing with what is real.

9. Don't Expect to be Happy Every Day

Happiness is an elusive thing. It comes at the most unexpected times. There are times that we think we should be happy and are not. We may strive to create a wonderful experience and fail miserably. Yet at other times we are filled with joy when we least expect it. Hold onto those precious times and savour them.

Don't search for happiness. Endeavour to help others to become happy and secure. Minor successes can be as rewarding as major ones.

Value your own contribution to the world however small it may seem to be. The sum total of countless little kindnesses always adds up to a wonderful contribution to mankind. We are all working together doing the part that we were made to do.

All the parts fit together like a jigsaw. Realise that your part is important and be content in your achievements. Do the best that you can do, always keeping in mind that your best will vary from day to day.

10. <u>Learn to laugh at yourself</u>

Learn to laugh at yourself. If you make silly mistakes or do something that you know you should not have done, don't try to justify yourself by doing a cover up job, offering some grand explanation, telling lies or blaming someone else. Admit you made the mistake, said the wrong thing or hurt someone's feelings and apologise. Hold up your hands and say it was you. This heals the breach immediately. It stops further hurts and the need to possibly tell more lies. Learn to admit your mistakes, correct them, learn from them and laugh at yourself for making them.

11. <u>Be a Forgiving Person</u>

Aim to be a forgiving person every minute of your life. Aim to view yourself in every aspect of you life. Be like an observer watching yourself in action:

- Develop self awareness.
- Be aware of other people.
- Be aware of how people interact.
- Be aware of how everything fits together.
- Mostly remember to see the "big picture".

If you do this you will see how you move, talk and interact with life. You will become very aware of self and the effect you have on the world. It is up to you now to ensure that it is a positive, loving, forgiving contribution. It is up to you to choose what sort of person you will be and to do all that is in your power to become that person. You were born to be a truly wonderful human being. Be all that you were born to be. Realise your potential.

12. <u>Patience and Tolerance</u>

Patience and tolerance are the two highest virtues. Certainly they are the most difficult to attain. Through daily forgiveness of self and others, through becoming a forgiving person patience and tolerance grow slowly within. Tranquillity begins to reign and joy seeps into the heart and mind. Moments of stillness are treasured. Good health is restored

*"What frightens me is that men
are content with what is
not life at all."*

Elizabeth Barrett Browning

Chapter 5

Causes of Unforgiveness

After working through the initial stages of the forgiveness process you will begin to apply the principles to your daily life. If you try to see the "big picture" all the time you begin to relate more easily to others as well as observing your own part. Self-awareness increases. The part you play becomes more meaningful and with this comes a willingness to change. If we understand this we can more easily forgive and take measures to protect ourselves from repeated hurts. Many things cause people to act the way they do.

1. <u>Assumptions</u>

We make assumptions about what other people think, do and say putting our own interpretations on actions and words. We also make assumptions based on how others dress, where they live, employment, accent, race, skin colour, looks etc. Frequently we make broad judgements and often reach the wrong conclusions. Perhaps it would be wiser to be guided more by our instinctive, intuitive sensing of the Being within, being more positively loving in our approaches and communicating more with the soul rather than the outward shell.

2. <u>Lack of communication</u>

Lack of true communication causes massive problems. Many people can only voice hurt or misunderstanding by arguing or raising voices. Everything said is taken as criticism. Hurtful things are said in anger thereby compounding the problem. An objective discussion is the best way forward with emotional responses avoided. This is a difficult thing to learn especially if there is a long history of immature quarrelling.

Try this:-
- Only one person needs to be different. This alters the whole balance and dynamics of the relationship.
- Choose to be calm and reasonable. You must make a commitment to yourself to do this at all times. It is not easy at first. Old habits will try to gain control. Do not allow this to happen. Persevere and you will be amazed at the change that occurs.
- Speak with a caring concern for others. You may not be fully understood at first but changes will soon begin to happen.
- Communication is important. Speak! Say what needs to be said.
- Take time to talk effectively.

Most people want every one else to change without realising that it is they who must initiate it. The resulting change in others may be slow but eventually the light will dawn. If you are different the pattern is broken. You have the chance to make life different. Be strong but beware; other people will try to suck you back into old behaviour patterns.

3. __Total Communication?__

No one fully understands you 100%. Everyone puts a personal interpretation on what you say, therefore you must come to understand that you will never be in total agreement with anyone neither will you ever be totally understood. You will agree on some points and not on others. The best that can be is a compromise. Decide what you do agree on and respect the rights of other individuals to differ.

4. __Rigid Thinking__

Many people find change difficult, even fearful. They like the familiar and will resist any suggestions for change no matter how beneficial these may be. For them it is easier to "keep driving the car". They may be stuck in a rut but it is a comfortable one, one that they know well. Changes to lifestyle demand sustained effort that many do not want to undertake. Some reasons for resisting change may be:–

- "This is what I/my family have always done."
- "This is what is expected of me. If I try to be different I will not be accepted in the social group I was born into/want to be in."
- "I feel safe like this. It's what I know best."
- "I don't like being challenged."
- "I don't have the knowledge, money, accent, clothes etc. to effect the change."
- "It's easier to do things this way.

- "I may be rejected if I become the person I would like to be."
- "Others will take my desire to change as a criticism of their way of life/values."
- "Stepping outside social boundaries is wrong."

Most people feel safe in set routines and refuse to change since they feel threatened by it and anyone who is, or wants to be, different. This often manifests itself in hostile behaviour, aggression, hurtful remarks and arguments.

5. Learned Behaviour Responses

Ways of dealing with situations are instilled in us throughout our childhood by the way our parents reacted to each other, other adults and to us. We observe as children the way adults manipulate situations and each other and we do the same as children and throughout our adult life. We continually re-enact situations, repeating the same words and body language that our parents used and the same methods of dealing with problems. We hang onto the same argument routines and depress ourselves since we never seem to move forward. We are stuck as if in a mouse-wheel destined to follow the same path forever **unless we choose to be different.**

Refuse to conform to the habitual behaviour patterns which dominate your life. Examine your behaviour. Note the things which trigger negative responses and change the way you react. Until you do this you are not in control of your life; not the person you know you can be. This takes practice therefore be patient with yourself.

6. Prejudices (racial, religious, class, social)

These are often historical i.e. passed on from generation to generation, formed by events long past; but the ingrained thought patterns and attitudes are clung to without question or review. In many cases the concepts are no longer relevant but are rarely challenged within the family/group. Any hint of change is usually strongly rejected.

7. Language

a. Words mean different things to different people e.g. love often means "Do what I want you to do"! This usually comes with the implication that love will be withdrawn if the correct response is not given.
No one fully understands exactly what another means verbally, since the concept of words varies from person to person, except for purely factual statements. Opinions, observations, emotions and beliefs are more difficult to convey

b. In almost all conversations, whether amicable or otherwise, most people focus on what directly affects or relates to them and do not absorb the whole concept. This inevitably causes confusion and, at times, it will seem as if one or other of the participants is not listening or, that two parallel subjects are being discussed. It could also signal disinterest, rejection, lack of love, boredom etc. and could lead to serious family disputes which build up walls of unforgiveness.

c. Some people do not remember what you say to them. You may think they are not interested or just did not bother to listen.

8. Fear

Fear builds up mistrust, which leads to resentment, which in turn leads to unforgiveness:

- Fear of not being accepted.
- Fear of being ostracized.
- Fear of peer pressure.
- Fear of the unknown.
- Fear of change.
- Fear of being unloved.
- Fear of being lonely.
- Fear of lack of security.
- Fear of lack of financial security.
- Fear of lack of education
- Fear of being misunderstood.
- Fear of revealing the true self.
- Fear of showing emotion.
- Fear of being bullied.
- Fear of being abused or assaulted.

9. Windows on the World

Everyone sees the world from his or her own perspective as if looking through a window. Some windows are very small i.e. a very narrow view of life. Others have larger windows and have a more open attitude. Yet again others are continually expanding their window including every experience, every moment and every opportunity that life presents.

The latter is the way forward to constant development. If the view of life is fiercely contained, forgiveness of others is difficult since seeing the big picture is impossible.

10. <u>Holding Grudges</u>

Holding a grudge long term is frequently thought of as a way of paying back a hurt. In a close relationship this is terribly damaging to all concerned. It is a futile act of punishment, which serves as no constructive solution. It can cause long-term problems perhaps leading to illness. Holding grudges and resentments drains an enormous amount of energy, which would be better used to maintain good health.

To hold a grudge against a person or persons that you rarely see is ludicrous. Most certainly the other people involved are not aware of your misery and are getting on with their own lives blissfully unaware of your hurts. Therefore the only person you are damaging is yourself. The best sort of payback is to forgive, learn the lesson that life was teaching you from the situation, let go and move on to a more successful, happy life

Being happy and enjoying your life, taking hold of all the opportunities that present themselves and having the strength to go forward, regardless of any further problems that may occur, is the best sort of payback

11. Long Term Abuse

This can mean sexual, emotional, physical or verbal at many different levels. Suffering is no respecter of person, sex, class or culture. Everyone suffers during their lives, some in more horrendous situations than others. Some are more able to rise above their suffering but the experience remains and needs to be dealt with.

Suffering should not be minimised just because others may have suffered more. It is a very personal torture of the soul and should be given sympathetic understanding at all levels and treated accordingly.

12. Bad Behaviour

Society in general accepts a variety of excuses for both adults and children behaving badly. Patterns of bad behaviour are often started in childhood and are continued into adulthood and by many into old age. Some people re-enact the same immature dramas all their lives obtaining more or less the same results. It may be that the result suits them and they behave badly to get what they want. Unfortunately in many situations the dramas are painful and the trauma increases with the years.

Some excuses for bad behaviour are:–

* illness, especially stress
* family problems
* someone has upset them
* loneliness
* accepted group behaviour i.e. peer pressure

- learned behaviour patterns from other family members/friends
- "that's the way I am" as if nothing can be or should be done to change it
- financial worries
- deprivation – emotional, physical, financial etc.
- discrimination in all its forms
- ignorance of a better way to behave
- refusal to acknowledge that there is a problem
- blaming someone else
- macho image
- fear of being rejected by cultural group for being different
- religious bigotry
- good behaviour patterns are totally alien i.e. don't know how to conduct themselves appropriately

13. Lack of Self Awareness

Many people do not realise the impact they have on the lives of those closest to them. They do not even think about how their behaviour can either enrich the lives of family and friends or damage it. To see the necessity is to take responsibility for your own actions influencing another person's state of mind, happiness and emotional welfare.

They are so preoccupied with thinking about themselves that they are neither aware nor caring of others. Other people then become tools to be used to supply their needs and wants. The unhappiness that this can cause is totally ignored as if it had nothing to do with them. This sort of person has neither self-awareness nor the ability to truly offer consideration. Everything they do is to satisfy their own needs and aspirations: self is totally important.

This may be because they are not in touch with their own emotions and cannot therefore empathise with anyone else's. It may be that the effects are noted but the person is unable to acknowledge responsibility. Or, they may feel unable to do anything about it because they don't know what to do!

Perhaps they think that it is up to each individual to find their own happiness. They are possibly unaware that interaction with others is a major factor in finding a balance in life, which leads to contentment and the opportunity to experience happiness and joy.

Constant friction is not good for your health. Denying a person the right to a peaceful, happy life is totally selfish and thoughtless.

14. Attention Seeking

Mannerisms, mode of speech and tone of voice may be un-knowingly cultivated to gain attention or achieve most impact. Frequently negative attention is seen to be better than none. People who are ignored or feel unloved often react badly to minor hurts to maximise the amount of attention they can acquire. This then becomes a normal response if allowed to continue.

15. Selfishness

This is, perhaps, the most obvious reason but one which may be over looked, since it is so rife. It is so ingrained in society that it is almost acceptable to "look after number one". This way of thinking is not a balanced way of dealing with life. This type of individual will constantly find themselves in situations where others people's needs must be taken into consideration. An unwillingness or point blank refusal to do so will cause friction in varying degrees.

You cannot live for self alone, expecting to have your own way all the time. It is a childish, extremely immature way of looking at life. Of course you must meet your own needs, but not to the exclusion of everyone else in your life. A balance can be found if you think about each situation carefully. Sometimes the focus will be on you and at other times on others. Compromises often have to be made. This can be done with no loss of dignity and a possible elevation in self esteem.

"When you think everything is hopeless a little ray if light comes from somewhere!"

Inscription in an inn,
St. Moritz, Switzerland

Chapter 6

The Forgiveness Process Stage 2

<u>Deeper Issues</u>

1. Some issues need deeper attention, simply because they have caused the deepest hurts, and these are the incidents that we have gone over and over in our minds. These are the things that just don't seem to want to go away.

2. These very deep and painful hurts need deeper more detailed examination. You must really put these pictures under a microscope and go through the forgiveness process as previously described in Stage 1 again, in minute detail.

3. Hold the picture of the event in your mind's eye and examine the faces, body language, clothing, speech, environment and the era in which the event occurred.

4. It is very important that you do this objectively. Try at all times to view each situation as an observer.

5. Often acceptable behaviour with one generation is totally different to what is acceptable with subsequent generations, therefore putting a different slant on any incident. It will also be different from family to family and even person to person within families. You must try to get things into context.

6. Consider these areas when thinking about past events:-

*   Age gaps – between parents and children and between siblings
*   Life experience
*   Financial status
*   Emotional deprivation or traumas
*   Intellectual capacity
*   Codes of practice perhaps related to family or work
*   Educational level
*   Upbringing
*   Character - selfish, distant, loving, happy, sad
*   Lifestyle
*   Cultural differences – regional, national, social
*   Religious beliefs – level of commitment

7. It is vital that you view the situations as an observer.

8. It is imperative that you work through the process objectively since becoming emotionally involved colours the memory and makes your examination biased.

9. This very deep forgiveness work will be very painful since you are addressing the very core of your being. You may become very upset, weepy, depressed etc.

10. You will find that there is much work to be done in changing your own attitudes to life, since we all have certainly played our own part in holding onto hurts for our own reasons. This must be taken on board.

Consider:–
- Pre-conceived ideas of how you think life should be or how the people in your life should act.
- Are you too easily offended?
- Do you have a St. Joan attitude i.e. want to save the world.
- Do you like to manipulate people? You may do this without realising that you are doing it.
- Is your approach to life too rigid?

11. Consider these possible reasons for holding back forgiveness:-
- You thought you were getting your own back on someone. Did you really? Did the person know that they had hurt you?
- You didn't want them to get away with it? Do you think the person or people concerned were even aware of the hurt caused? Even if they were or still are, you are allowing others to control your life. If you forgive them they lose their power over you.
- You just didn't know how to deal with it? If you can see the whole picture you can often see a solution.

12. Tackle each issue as it comes to mind.

13. Be very determined. Take the time it takes. Don't try to rush the process.

14. When you have covered all the big hurts deal with any other memories that come to mind. Remember this is a continuing process not a one-off fix.

15. When you have dealt with everything that you can remember, declare that you absolutely forgive everyone and anything that has ever caused you pain. Open your arms wide and say aloud:

"I forgive you and I let it all go".

16. Now make positive thinking a habit. Refuse to think about the negative aspects of your life. Think of the present and the future and leave the past behind.

"We are continually faced with great opportunities brilliantly disguised as problems."

Mark Twain

"Experience is the name everyone gives to their mistakes."

Oscar Wilde

Chapter 7

The Forgiveness Process Stage 3

<u>Next Steps</u>

1. Forgiveness must now become an integral part of your everyday life. Try to forgive as situations arise that upset you in any way. Certainly take time at the end of each day to clear your thoughts of any traces of resentment.

2. You may think that nothing has happened that day that you need to deal with. If this is the case make a blanket forgiveness statement that covers anything that might, in any way, cause the least trace of a problem.

3. Say, "I forgive anyone who may have caused me hurt by word, deed, thought, attitude or look. I forgive them and I let it go." This covers anything that may have slipped in subconsciously or unnoticed.

4. If you do this, it keeps your level of unforgiveness as low as possible and prevents the build up that caused the problems originally.

5. Now think of the way you interact with people. There will be characteristics that you need to adjust or change completely to accommodate your new way of thinking.

6. There will be habitual responses to daily routines, conversations and arguments that have followed the same

patterns for years. This needs to change to ensure that the same resentments are not allowed to accumulate.

7. Do not allow anyone to treat you in any way that diminishes you as a valuable person. You have a right to be treated with dignity and respect. The challenge is to treat every one else the same way.

8. The people you live with are accustomed to you behaving in a particular way, a way that they are familiar with and to responding in their usual fashion. If you start to act differently this may come as shock.

9. Old habits are hard to break. It takes determination and not a little work but, if you want life to be different, you must do something to make it different yourself.

10. " A journey of a thousand miles begins with one step." Be brave. Make a start. Do a little at a time.

11. Life may seem more difficult to begin with. Making major change is never easy. Be patient.

12. As you become stronger, your family and friends will come to accept the changes as normal and begin to treat you differently.

"Nurture great thoughts for you will never go higher than your thoughts."

Benjamin Disraeli

Chapter 8

The Way Forward

1. Acknowledge the person you are

Peer pressure, in all its various forms, tries to push us into conforming to group ideals to the extent that people feel so obliged to be alike that they lose any feeling of self. They do not know who they really are, so habitually have they followed the set rules and values of a group or ideology. The true self has been obliterated.

Sit down in a quiet place and think about what you really, in your heart of hearts, think and feel about yourself and life. Have the courage to follow your own instincts. Acknowledge yourself and begin to live the way you truly wish to. It is not easy at first. Old habits die hard. If you are determined, you will gradually change and become the person that you were meant to be.

If you acknowledge yourself in this way, you can then acknowledge the true being in others. To do this you must treat yourself and others with tolerance, patience, dignity and kindness.

2. You Are Not Alone

Know that you are not alone in your frailty. No one escapes. The problem is that so few people are willing to admit to failure or feelings of defeat. The majority only talk of success, happy times, successful careers, lives and families. Few admit to the trials, disappointments and hardships of living for fear of being labelled as unable to cope.

Successful living is overcoming these very trials and stoically going on believing that life has meaning and purpose. Everyone has problems. You are not different. You are not alone in feeling miserable, depressed or isolated at various points in your life. It is the holding on and going forward that is important.

Believe in the beauty of life; believe that you will get through your trials, and joy will come again. It is only through experiencing sorrow and hitting low points that you are able to appreciate the exhilaration of success and overwhelming gratitude of being alive.

3. Be Honest With Yourself

Many people are not honest with themselves or those they come in contact with. They deceive themselves by justifying words and actions, minimising the fault as if it was of no account. Even small deceptions are accountable since collectively they become something bigger. Dishonesty comes in many forms:–

- Deliberate lies
- Covering up
- Putting up a front
- Political correctness

These may seem insignificant. You may say everyone does it and feel justified. Everyone hides behind this excuse. Just because *everyone* does something does not make it right, *or* acceptable, *or* even a good reason to be the same. Think for yourself. Millions of people hide their true selves behind curtains of pretence, acting out a part, making a sham of life by denying their true personality.

Cast aside the habits of dishonesty and pretence. Have the courage to acknowledge your true self. You *are* "good enough". You will feel more comfortable in your skin and become more open with others. Above all be honest with yourself. No matter how hard you try, you cannot make yourself the same as another person.

Stop being hard on yourself. Let go of the demands of society, peer groups, family and friends. If you can acknowledge yourself, you can begin to acknowledge others and become a more dignified, more caring human being.

4. Who You Are Now

You are different now to the person you were in previous years.
Consider this:–

* You can be a series of people e.g. child, teenager, parent, employee, middle-aged adult, older adult, teacher, shop assistant etc.
* As you move through life you constantly change, becoming a composite individual.
* As an adult can you be held responsible for the decisions you made and the circumstances you found yourself in at every stage of your life?

- As you grow older, need you carry the same image of yourself throughout the years?
- Is it healthy and intelligent to fiercely stick to the same attitudes throughout your life?
- Surely we should leave these other selves behind like old friends who have taught us great lessons and move on, accepting who we have become.
- Too many people live with regrets and trail them behind like an enormous burden when they can leave them behind.
- Many people wish for a time in their lives that is long past instead of living in the present. They waste life by living with memories of either happier or sadder times.
- Still others continually plan ahead and live in the future. While it is good to plan ahead this should not diminish the present.
- Enjoy memories but live in the day, the moment you are in right now.

5. <u>Don't Keep Taking it on the Chin</u>

You may have successfully forgiven the past and the people concerned, including yourself, but you should not feel obliged to keep taking further injustices. For a large part of my life this what I thought forgiveness was all about. I thought that taking it on the chin, turning the other cheek and forgiving was all that had to be done. I wondered why I kept repeatedly being hurt but did not know the solution. After I discovered the forgiveness process, I found the part that I had missed i.e. how to stop the hurts. I realised I did not and should not keep taking it on the chin!

So try these suggestions:-

- Learn to say "No". Don't be persuaded to do things that you truly do not want to do.
- Say what you mean and mean what you say, but think carefully first.
- Identify what you want to do. Don't become involved in situations that you would prefer not to be in.
- Stay out of other people's arguments.
- Be firm about what you will or will not do.
- Don't allow anyone to abuse you in any way – physically, emotionally, mentally or spiritually. Zero tolerance.
- Respect yourself and expect respect from other people.
- Act like the strong person you want to be. Be very determined.
- Value yourself.
- Choose the kind of person you want to be and make the necessary changes.
- Decide what you need to do to make it happen. Make a plan and work the plan.

6. Take Your Place

Too many people wait for others to give them the attention that they would like. Instead of naturally taking part, they think that they should be invited or included in some way. The result is frequently a feeling of exclusion leading to feelings of resentment.

Don't wait on others to give you "your place" Take it. Make an effort to be sociable by showing an interest in everyone and everything. Be as kind and helpful as possible. Stand up for what you believe in. You have a right to a voice, to be listened to. You have a right to be acknowledged.

7. Find a balance to Your Life

Considering self is frequently linked with selfishness. However this depends on the balance in your life. Everyone needs time to recharge their batteries, relax or enjoy hobbies. Too much time devoted to self inevitably means that you do not include other people sufficiently. The other side of the coin is that you consider others too much; you lose sight of yourself and your own needs and begin to feel used. Your own feeling of identity is lost. You then become a tool for others to make use of. It becomes difficult to extricate yourself from either position to find the right balance.

Thinking too much of self leads to narrow thinking and lack of true love and compassion for others. Thinking too little leads to loss of self-esteem and a true realisation of your own talents and potential.

Society tries to fix us in traditional roles making it difficult to find our own focus and balance. Think carefully about your deepest needs and aspirations and balance this against what others would have you do. Denial of self is not good for the soul. Have the courage to become an achiever, setting aside time to gain successes no matter how small. Your closest family and friends may be surprised. Perhaps it suits them to have you consider them first all the time. But, remember, you have a place, hopes, dreams and rights to be considered.

8. Importance Levels

Sort out what is important in your life. You may place too much importance on matters that are low level. This does not mean that these items do not need dealt with but it does mean that you should get things into perspective. Don't make a big deal out of everything. You will exhaust yourself and everyone around you. Don't use up your thinking time on other people and problems. Get a balance to your life. Think of it like a dimmer switch i.e. some problems need to take top priority, some low priority and others at varying importance levels.

Find other things to think about, for example, a hobby that you can focus on. Direct your thinking power to something enjoyable. Don't drain your energy on fruitless worrying.

9. Clean Out

Get rid of items that trigger bad memories. Anything that reminds you of a bad experience with a person or incident needs to be removed from your life. Every time you look at these items you will recall the pain even though you have forgiven. It is best to give yourself the best opportunity to move on with your life by putting the past behind and living in the present. Nurture good memories.

10. <u>Stay Out of Other Peoples' Disputes</u>

Don't become embroiled in other peoples' disputes. You may find yourself blamed or misunderstood by either party. If you feel you must comment be calm, constructive, impartial and objective. Do not become emotionally involved. *If in doubt, stay out*. Walk away if things become difficult!

11. <u>You Cannot Totally Depend on Anyone</u>

Factual certainty is not applicable to personal relationships since so many variables come into play at different levels, mainly emotional. Therefore there is always the climate for misunderstanding and hurt if you look for things to be different. Be prepared to make allowances.

.

13. <u>The Same Old Road</u>

Choose not to think about the things that hurt. If you have completed the forgiveness process, try to break the old habit of thinking about the same incidents again and again. This takes practice but you can do it. Cultivate instead the new habit of positive thinking, choosing a balanced approach to life and think about what really matters. Enjoy each day as much as possible given the unpredictability of life.

14. <u>Victim?</u>

Don't think of yourself as a victim. You may not realise that you think this way. However, if you have reached a way of thinking that makes you feel that there is nothing you can do to change your life, or your problems, you may have a victim complex. You may think that you must accept the way that others treat you even although you are unhappy. This is not so. Begin by visualising how you would like life to be then make a plan. Change things in small ways always working toward your goal. Don't give up. Change little things you do and say. Change the way you treat others and the way you allow them to treat you. Eventually things will start to change. If you are different then everyone around you will gradually change too.

15. <u>Hobbies</u>

Develop hobbies and interests where the groups of people are the same type as you, speak in the same mode, are interested in the same things and are willing to accept you readily into the group. If you are unhappy in any situation move, leave the unhappiness behind and move on. You will be surprised at what life has in store if only you are brave enough to do it.

16. <u>Life is Not Perfect</u>

Long held beliefs about how life should be, culled from childhood experiences, culture, parents, family and friends, form our ideas of how we would like to shape our own lives. We somehow think that we can form our own perfect life by correcting all the mistakes that our parents, family and friends have made. We convince ourselves that we are going to make life the way we want it to be. In our naivety, we worry, fret and strive to complete the picture we have formed, forgetting that there is more than one person involved. Unless the other people in our lives know and agree to our plan, our dream can never be accomplished. We strive in vain.

Reality is not what we want to accept. We tell ourselves if only this or that happened or he/she would do/say/become then life would be perfect. The people in our lives are not puppets for us to manoeuvre at will. They too have their thoughts and dreams which almost certainly differ from yours. So set realistic plans and learn to live with reality.

17. Keep Your Personal Space

Don't allow others too close to you all the time otherwise you cannot remain objective. You end up emotionally drained and buffeted by the demands and problems of all and sundry.
We all need love, attention and communication but not all the time. Strike a balance. Decide who to be close to, when, and how close you want to be. For most of the time we should retain a comfortable physical, emotional and mental distance, even with friends and family, in order to function efficiently, be objective and conserve emotional energy. The amount of closeness in each area will also vary depending on circumstances.

18. Don't Be Confrontational

If you know that a certain look, word, phrase or action triggers a negative response, don't do it! Choose a different way of handling the circumstances or don't broach the subject at all. Avoid the prospect of creating an unhappy situation.

Take into consideration the fact that people develop at varying rates in every area, not only physically and academically but emotionally and spiritually, and be compassionate toward them.

Life is a constant confrontation with choice. Get your priorities right. What is more important, some old argument or hurt, or present day peace and contentment.

"The unexamined life is not worth living."

Socrates

"God did not give us a spirit of timidity but a spirit of power and love and self-control."

2 Timothy ch.1 v.7

Chapter 9

A Second Chance

I have travelled a long way since beginning the search for forgiveness: forgiveness for myself, and the ability to forgive others. It has been difficult but so amazing and so worthwhile. I feel today more completely *me* than I have ever felt before. I have discovered a path to freedom, a way to be more loving, a way to say "Yes" and "No" without feeling guilty and an acceptance of life and the people in my life.

I know myself better and accept who I am. I *like* me. My health has vastly improved. Most of the time the terrifying vertigo and imbalance appears to have been a bad dream. Then it comes to visit me as a reminder not to take life for granted. Forgiveness is not the only discipline that has needed to be learned. Many things have contributed to the improvement in my health.

1. A rigorous physiotherapy programme of head and neck exercises was followed over several months. These were designed to re-educate my brain to accept head movements and had to be practised a minimum of twice a day. I managed to do most of them but there were some that I just could not, and still cannot, do. This I willingly accept since I realise that I can never go back to the way I was before my illness began. Along with the health limitations has come more than I could ever have dreamed possible.

2. My neck needs to be manipulated regularly since the spondylitis is still there and always will be.

3. During the first year of consultations with my holistic physician, I had various treatments and regularly took homeopathic medicine and other remedies. I have continued to do this at varying intervals since.

4. A detox programme had to be implemented to clear my body of toxins and gallstones. This involved taking a monthly concoction over a period of eight months initially and repeated as required.

Good health practices concerning food and exercise are essential to wellness. It is wise to give the body the best chance of recovery. Here are some of the things that I had to do and continue to do:-

Food
- Eat organic food as much as possible. This helps to limit the build up of toxins in the body.
- My body reacts badly to dairy products, mustard, chocolate, cola, cocoa and alcohol. All of these foods were therefore eliminated from my diet.
- Eat a high proportion of fruit and vegetables.
- Eat only freshly prepared food.
- Eliminate all junk food i.e. crisps, carry out meals, fizzy drinks etc.

Water Drink plenty of water to keep the body hydrated, to flush out toxins and to aid elimination. I drink two glasses first thing in the morning then two half an hour before each meal with extra taken as required e.g. after exercise or in warm weather.

Exercise   Get sufficient exercise to keep the body fit and healthy. I try to be as active as possible ensuring that I take regular exercise each week. When walking, routes where there is heavy traffic are avoided so that exhaust fumes are not inhaled. Walks in parks and countryside are preferred.

Cigarette Smoke   I avoid people and situations where I may encounter it. I react badly to cigarette smoke therefore in hotels and restaurants I make a point of asking for smoke free facilities. The effects of passive smoking are now well documented.

Fresh Air   Breathe fresh air. Ensure that your home is aired each day. Open the windows in each room of the house to change the air even in winter, if only for a short time.

Relaxation   Learn to breathe well by filling the lungs completely with oxygen. Most people are shallow breathers and fail to oxygenate their bodies properly. Slow deep breathing can also help to relax you. I include this in my routine of simple relaxation exercises.

Sleep   Maintain a routine sleep pattern. Aim to be in bed at the same time each night and rise at the same time each day. This trains your body to sleep well during this period. There may be occasions when this is not possible e.g. special nights out, but always return to the routine pattern immediately.

Overwork   Finding a balance between doing and being has been difficult. For a large part of my life I worked full time, reared a family, kept a large house immaculately clean, looked after parents, decorated the house and tried to have the kind of social life that I thought I was entitled to since I worked so hard. No wonder I was always tired and eventually became ill. No one can be busy twenty-four/seven year in and year out and not suffer some consequences. Nowadays I am much stricter with myself. I endeavour to organise my days to allow for "Me" time, always being aware of the need for a balance between activity and relaxation, work and pleasure.

Positive Thinking Be careful what you think! I told myself every day that I was well even when it was obvious that I was not. I talked myself into a frame of mind whereby I totally expected to be well. I assumed that good health was mine. I claimed it for myself. From thinking of myself as a sick woman to the opposite was an amazing boost to my feeling of well being. It was the drive I needed to keep the other disciplines in place.

These are the basic building blocks that I used. Good health is something I value therefore I will maintain these disciplines and, if applicable, add any others that I read about or am told of. I shall not be going back to my old life style; after all, that is how I became sick in the first instance.

This is my second chance. I willingly accept the challenges that this entails. It has been an amazing voyage of discovery. It has changed my whole way of thinking about life. It has set my spirit free.

"The man who believes he can do something is probably right, and so is the man who believes he can't."

Anonymous

"A wise man should consider that health is the greatest of human blessings, and learn how by his own thoughts to derive benefits from his illness."

Hippocrates

Chapter 10

As Life Goes On

Once you can readily forgive on a daily basis, once forgiveness becomes a natural part of your Being you can begin to focus your energies on what is really important in your life. Energy is constantly drained by becoming uptight about the petty trivia, the "who said what" and the mindfulness of ones own little hangups. When you can see the wider picture you can see where you fit into the world. You can take your place with confidence. You can feel the assurance that your choices are *right for you* and not dictated by the emotional conflict thrust upon you by others. You can stand back and view your way forward, the path you want to walk, with a feeling of rightness. And because of this you have the ability to be kind, gracious, generous and respectful of those around you. You can sympathise with their problems and in some measure help them toward solutions.

There may be times when you feel uncertain. Take time to think things through carefully so that the decisions you make are chosen by reasoned response and the feeling of, "this is right for me and it fits".

When problems arise take time to deal with them effectively. Don't try to sweep them under the carpet or bury your head in the sand in the vain hope that they will disappear. Don't let anxiety, anger and resentment build up. Find solutions as quickly as possible. If you are unable to do this yourself go to someone whom you think can offer assistance. Apply the remedy and practise any necessary forgiveness. If you do this daily for all problems, no matter how small, you keep your life free from the annoying irritations that seep happiness, love, joy and energy from your life.

From time to time you may have to face a major life event which knocks all your hard won peace and calm awry. This happened to me quite recently with the death of a sibling. Although the death was not unexpected it still turned my life upside down. Childhood memories came flooding back. Things I had previously had no recollection of pounded through my brain. It was as if a tidal wave of thoughts, impressions, emotions and mental pictures was about to engulf me. I was paralysed by guilt and punished myself by thinking of all the things that I could have done differently. It was totally confusing to find myself in this situation considering all the work I had done on forgiveness.

Eventually the numbness began to wear off and I started the forgiveness process as described in this book. It was effective with the bulk of the problems but there was one area that I could not seem to solve. No matter how much I tried I could not find a reasonable conclusion. I puzzled over this for some weeks before I realised that the person I needed to forgive was someone whom I had particularly loved and admired. I had thought this individual to be above reproach. Deep down inside me I had not wanted it to be this person so had blanked out the possibility of considering them.

Once I recognised the problem, I could see that this individual was connected to so many other incidents. I had to start the forgiveness process again and include this person in all the different stages. Now the "big picture" started to make sense. It became clearer and more meaningful. When I said: "I forgive you and let it all go" a feeling of heaviness left me each time. The burden of sadness and guilt went stage by stage until I could truly say that I felt free.

To a lesser degree, the same sort of thing happened a few months later when a childhood friend died. Memories that had been locked away for tens of years resurfaced; many of them happy and funny and others that brought heartache. As always at these times regret visits with the accompanying guilt. How do you deal with all of this? Certainly have a time of mourning but then move on to forgiveness where necessary.

Especially in these instances, the final part must certainly be a remembrance of the happy times. Gratitude for the lessons learned from these special people and the joy and happiness shared.

There will be other times in my life when life events will trigger series of memories: some happy and some painful. This is the very nature of being alive. It is not the problem that is the important issue. It is how you deal with it. If you have strategies for handling situations you have the tools to move on successfully, to learn, to move forward, to face new changes and accept new challenges. Life is a learning process. The next hurdle is just around the corner.

No matter how well planned your existence is, there is always the possibility of disruption at some level. We cannot foretell exactly how people will react in a given situation. There is always the unexpected to deal with, the "chaos factor". The best we can do is to plan effectively while aiming to be flexible at the same time. If you can accept this, there is less likelihood of building up stress, anger and resentment. Life is not perfect and, no matter how hard you try, you will not make it so. Don't try to be perfect yourself or expect perfection from anyone else. Strive for high standards but don't beat yourself into the ground if you fall short or make mistakes. Learn from the experience and move on.

The burden of unforgiveness and its accompanying feelings drain the body of energy causing tiredness, headaches, depression etc. Letting go allows the energy spent on these fruitless pursuits to be maximised for more pleasant emotions and activities. At every stage of forgiveness, no matter how trivial or how overwhelming the issue to be dealt with, I invariably feel an upsurge of energy when I have completed the process. It amazes me each time it happens.

"Judge not, that you be not judged. For with the judgement you pronounce you will be judged, and the measure you give will be the measure you get. Why do you see the speck that is in your brother's eye, but do not notice the log that is in your own eye?"

Matthew 7 v 1-2

Chapter 11

What is forgiveness?

What is forgiveness?

- It is a conscious act of will which one makes to release the suffocating grip of past hurts.
- It is choosing to let go and move on.
- It is choosing to be different.
- It is regaining control over your life.
- It is accepting reality i.e. people make mistakes, accidents happen. That's life!
- It is giving others the gift of forgiveness.
- It is the peace you find when you release negative feelings.
- It is not using others as reasons for our own failures.
- It is taking responsibility for our own actions/mistakes/failings.
- It is not hiding from our own inadequacies.
- It is learning from life's experiences.
- It is making decisions about the future based on these lessons.
- It is healing yourself.

What replaces all the hurt and negativity?

The space must be filled otherwise the demons come back to haunt us.

It is filled by:-

- an awareness of the fragility of life.
- the knowledge that no one is perfect.
- compassion for others who are obviously not in control of their emotions.
- acceptance that the past is in the past and you are free to live in the now.
- the assurance that you have a means of managing present and future traumas.
- a purposeful attitude to life.
- accepting new challenges with confidence.
- developing your own ideas, talents and relationships.
- living with reality, not with how you think life *should* be.

You may feel that there are certain things that you need to do to complete the process, to draw a line under the past.

You may want to:-

- search for a lost relative.
- put flowers at someone's grave.
- visit a friend from the past.
- visit an area that you once lived in.
- give a donation to a relevant charity.
- apply for the college course you feel you missed out on.
- return an item that you took by mistake.
- do some voluntary work.

When problems occur

1. adopt a non-judgemental attitude.
2. immediately forgive.

3. decide what part you play in it.
4. examine the situation to discover what life is trying to teach you.
5. if you need help, seek out the best qualified person.
6. do what needs to be done to solve the problem.
7. move on.

Forgiveness does not mean that all the hurtful things that have happened to you were justified in any way. It does not mean that the people who hurt you had a right to do what they did; but it does mean that the hold that these people and events had over your life has been removed. It is not about forgetting that something happened; but it is about refusing to remain a victim of these circumstances. It is not denying that the events occurred; but it is a refusal to allow your whole life to be scarred by them.

Everyone needs to learn how to forgive effectively, some more desperately than others. Those people who have a great need to forgive usually think about their problem areas with amazing regularity. They will also complain about these same things, frequently blaming particular people for all the problems they encounter. Their minds are occupied by the opinions that they think other people have of them. Their thoughts are dominated by the mistakes of the past.

In today's world there is an enormous pressure on everyone to perform and to conform to certain standards, instead of each individual listening to the inner self and feeling free to be guided by intuition. In order to do either of these you need to de-clutter your mind of all the junk that prevents you from functioning at optimum level. Learning to forgive keeps the channels free.

If you have accepted the challenge outlined in the previous chapters of this book, you will already be aware of changes in your life. You will feel less stressed, less depressed, less easily annoyed, more in control of your emotions and your life.

People are human. Human beings make mistakes. We offend and are offended usually because we do not have the tools to handle situations effectively. However, there is no need to punish ourselves again and again for the rest of our lives because of past incidents. Learn the forgiveness process. Learn the tool that brings peace to your life. Give yourself and the people in your life the gift of forgiveness. Become a forgiving person.

Summary of "The Forgiveness Process"

Summary of "The Forgiveness Process"

1. Make time each day to go to a quiet place to think over the different areas of your life. Ensure that you will not be disturbed. You may want to-
- take the phone off the hook.
- lock the door.
- close the curtains.
- curl up in a favourite chair.
- lie in a relaxation position.
- light a candle.

2. Take yourself as far back in time as you can remember and gradually move forward recalling as much detail as you can. When you come to anything that disturbs you spend more time picturing the exact details as accurately as you can. Close your eyes and visualise the moment, re-experience the pain and then move back and view the incident as an objective observer. Look at the whole picture, not just the little bit that applies to you. Examine the scene in your mind's eye looking at the reactions of everyone concerned.

3. Try to understand the situation as the person you are now. You may see possible reasons that will offer an explanation as to why the incident occurred. Remember to be rational and objective.

4. If possible tell a close friend about the incident. If there is no one available or you would rather not tell anyone about a particular incident, speak aloud to yourself. It is important to do this even if you are alone in an empty room. It is cleansing to finally get rid of all the rubbish that has been held inside for so long.

5. Make the decision to forgive everyone involved, including yourself even if you cannot understand the reasons why. Open your arms wide and say aloud,

"I forgive you and I let it all go".

6. Go through this process with each stage of your life. Don't try to skip over anything. Be meticulous in your work. Some incidents may require deeper thinking if they still appear to be a cause for concern. In these instances apply the forgiveness process again, looking for more detail.

7. Now apply the same procedure but, this time, think about all the happy times in your life. *Don't omit this part.* It is important to spend an equal amount of time on it. This will complete the process on a positive note and balance your thinking.

8. Now choose to be a forgiving person for the rest of your life dealing with problems on a daily basis.

9. Do what is necessary to change your life so that you can become the person you would like to be.

Examples

(All names have been changed to preserve confidentiality)

Example 1

Fred and his brother had been playing in an upstairs room. They had a disagreement and started to quarrel. Their voices became so loud that they woke their father who had been asleep in the next room. When he came through to the two boys he was very angry and immediately chastised Fred. Meanwhile his brother took the opportunity to escape.

When he reviewed this scenario Fred immediately forgave his brother as he could see that it was merely a childish squabble. However he had some difficulty forgiving his father since he thought that his brother had escaped being punished. This he thought was totally unfair because his own punishment had been harsh. When he revisited the scene Fred became very upset when he pictured the faces of the people involved. He felt the same overwhelming urge to escape at the memory of his father's angry face and the enormous sense of injustice at, as he thought, being the only one punished. However, when he managed to look at the scene as an observer, he could see the possible reason why his father was so easily angered. He was an insomniac and although he took sleeping pills regularly, he still did not get sufficient sleep. Most certainly he was exhausted and, being awakened when he had finally managed to sleep, was triggered into a rage.

When he realised this, Fred could hardly believe that he had held onto the hurt for so long. The difference now was that he was viewing the interaction with the eyes and mind of an adult, not a hurt little boy. Forgiveness was a welcome release.

Some weeks later, when he happened to talk about this incident with his brother, he discovered that he had also been punished, but in a different part of the house. Fred had nursed the wrong information for most of his adult life!

Fred's father had been a very harsh, dictatorial parent who would lose his temper easily. He had subsequently developed the same attitude to himself. He was very hard on himself, avoided confrontations and was easily upset. Once Fred began to see the "big picture" he could see the possible difficulties that his father may have had to cope with. Family disputes, money worries, lack of sleep and long-term illness were some of the things that his father struggled with on a daily basis. As an adult, with a family of his own, viewing these events he could empathise with his father. He could see that perhaps he had difficulty coping with some situations and had reacted unwisely. Each generation has different attitudes to child rearing. He accepts that his father did the best he knew how at that particular time in his life.

With acceptance of his father came an understanding of his own behaviour patterns. He could see the reasons why he acted and felt the way he did. Now he could leave these events in the past and move on with more confidence. His emotional health is more balanced, he has learned to be gentle with himself, to face problems, find solutions and move on. Fred's relationship with his brother has also improved. The long held feelings of injustice have gone and in their place a warm friendship has grown.

Example 2

Jim had always felt angry with his parents because he was not given the opportunity to remain at school in order to gain the necessary qualifications to access further education at college or university. He was made to leave school as soon as he was fifteen and expected to find a job right away. Since he felt under pressure, lacked experience and was given no guidance, he chose a job that neither suited his ability level nor his temperament. This was to have an impact on the way he thought about and conducted the whole of his life.

When he thought over this situation, he discovered many contributing factors that he had never thought of before. He looked at all the people involved, thinking of what was happening in their lives to possibly make them talk and act the way they had. He visualised each of them, remembering what they looked like, what they wore, what they said, how they acted and where each incident occurred. He allowed himself to feel the emotions that he had felt at that time. He felt the pain and tried to feel the mood of the situation. He then moved back to the position of objective observer to examine what he saw and, in doing so, began to see the deeper implications. With the benefit of life experience and maturity, he could understand the possible adult problems involved that he could not possibly have begun to comprehend as a teenager.

His father had on going medical problems that necessitated time off work. Also he was unable to work the long hours required to earn the amount the family needed to live comfortably. His elder brother, who had been working for several years, left home to start a new job. This meant that his wage was not available to help support the family. His mother had recently had a baby, a late child. Extra funds were needed to provide the necessary equipment for the baby. She was also in poor health for many months.

Jim was now able to think of this situation with the adult maturity he now has instead of the immature, emotional response that he has carried around with him all his life. Now that he could see the possible reasons why, he could finally forgive and let go. In fact he felt proud of himself for the contribution he had made to the family at that time.

This realisation made an enormous difference to Jim's perception of himself. Since his teenage years he had thought of himself as being a "lesser" being since his parents had not valued him enough to give him a good education. He had equated this in his mind as:

- They did not love him.
- They did not think him intelligent.
- They thought more of his younger siblings who went into higher education.
- They found him unworthy in some way.
- He was different.

He had carried this feeling of worthlessness throughout his life. It had made him very aggressive, quick-tempered, domineering and self-opinionated. Once he realised the possible reasons for his parent's decision and the massive contribution he may have made to his family's life, these feelings of inadequacy and the behavioural traits that went with them began to fade.

Jim is now a more tranquil, considerate personality who is at peace with himself now that he feels worthy of love and respect. He knows he is an intelligent, knowledgeable human being.

Example 3

David and Susan met when they were both in their twenties. They were instantly attracted to each other and, after a whirlwind courtship, decided to get married just six months after they met. At this point they were faced with fierce opposition from David's mother and brother. The rest of the family appeared to approve. The reasons given were that they should get to know one another a bit better, wait a bit longer and save up for a fancy wedding and a nice home. David and Susan did not want to wait since they were quite happy with a quiet wedding and thought that they could pool their wages and save hard once they were married.

The wedding went ahead. The happy couple went on to make both a success of the marriage and their careers. Unfortunately David's mother and brother maintained their air of disapproval and frequent open animosity for many years. David and Susan were not included in family gatherings since the animosity was adopted by other family members.

This situation caused years of unhappy incidents which David and Susan found difficult to accept or understand.

When they reviewed the history of the affair they looked at each person involved and tried to understand why each individual may have developed the attitude that they did.

Mother:-

- She was afraid for her son thinking that he was rushing into a relationship that could cause him heartache.

- She was prejudiced against Susan because Susan's family were socially different.
- She was accustomed to getting her own way.
- She had extremely fixed views of life.

Brother:-

- He was older than David and still unmarried.
- He was very protective of him.
- He too was accustomed to getting his own way.
- He had a very forceful personality.

David and Susan had to accept that these two people had to be forgiven because, on examining the facts, it was apparent that neither personality had the ability or knowledge to effect change. Both of them remained the same fierce defenders of their right to say exactly as they thought, regardless of the hurts inflicted on other people.

David and Susan decided that there was no likelihood of change in these two people therefore they would have to make any changes themselves. A decision was made to limit the amount of time spent in their company but to always treat them with love and respect. In this way the impact of their unreasonable behaviour would be limited minimising possible emotional confrontations. During the occasional meetings, David and Susan endeavoured to remain as calm and controlled as possible so that the thoughtless remarks fired at them had minimal impact. These two family members had lost their power to hurt, dominate or manipulate.

Example 4

When George started his new job he was confident that he would be happy in his new environment. He looked forward to meeting new people, developing his career prospects and making new friends. On the first day it soon became apparent that things might not proceed as he had hoped. At the first team meeting no one spoke to him. Everyone appeared distant. As time went on it became apparent that he had been "sent to Coventry". George slowly became more and more depressed.

However he decided to work hard at his job learning as much as he could and gained an amazing amount of expertise. The original team members moved on and were replaced by new people who were more inclined to be friendly. Gradually life improved for George as he began to be accepted. Although his new colleagues thought well of him George was still affected by past treatment. His confidence and self-esteem had been damaged. He needed to forgive his former work mates in order to regain a balance in his life.

When he looked back at this phase he had many people to consider. He carefully thought of each individual, taking time to remember exactly what each person looked like and how they acted towards him. He tried to remember what was said in the conversations that he had overheard, trying to piece together possible reasons for their behaviour.

These are the conclusions he came to:-

- George had been appointed to a position that had been coveted by a former staff member.
- He was to have been considered for management training.
- He had a more prosperous life style than most of his new team members.
- He worked harder than the rest of the team.
- They did not want to work at George's level.

He came to see that the whole team was manipulated by peer pressure. There was a core few who pulled the strings and made the rules. Everyone was afraid to be different or to befriend him in case they were ostracized as well.

Although successful at work, George had gradually become more withdrawn, he did not attempt to join in conversations, his self-esteem plummeted and he felt very lonely. In a brave attempt to combat these feelings he worked harder, which pleased management but made the divide between George and his colleagues wider.

Forgiving this group of people had a dramatic effect on his life as he suddenly realised that many of the people who had excluded him were no longer part of the work force. The remaining members of staff were more amiable. This was his chance to be different. Once he released the hurts and resentment he felt free to be happy and responsive. Very quickly he became accepted as a valuable team member who was sought out for advice and help on a variety of projects. His self-esteem soared as he started to enjoy the level of contribution he could make.

Appendixes

Appendix A

Other Symptoms of Benign Paroxysmal Positional Vertigo

1.   Face often white and waxy. Sometimes yellowish.
2.   Feeling of pressure inside my head plus muzzy feeling.
3.   Head feels "too heavy ".
4.   Can't look or move head from side to side or up and down without feeling dizzy.
5.   Unable to focus eyes at times.
6.   Feel as if head is wobbling about when it is actually still.
7.   Inside of body feels as if it is trembling when it is actually still.
8.   Looking at other people looking up makes me feel dizzy.
9.   Moving my head during group conversations makes me feel ill. I usually try to position myself to ensure minimum head movement.
10. When dizzy spells come on I often feel terribly hot.
11. Lack concentration at times.
12. Poor memory at times.
13. Difficulty with steps. I need to hold onto a rail and look to the side when going down stairs.
14. Don't like bright lights.
15. Feel sick when travelling by car. Not good at longish distances especially if the road has too many bends or the car is moving at higher speeds.
16. Don't like bright or flashing lights or bright sunlight.
17. Flashing pictures on T.V. make me feel dizzy.
18. Feel tired all the time.
19. Often completely exhausted.

20. Often feel as if I'm going to fall forward or backward.
21. Can't stand on one spot for too long without holding on to something or moving about.
22. Patterned floors or stairs make me feel dizzy.
23. Head and neck often ache. Sometimes really painful.
24. Don't like people or objects too close to me. It makes me feel off balance.
25. Head never feels clear.
26. I need a good space round me, or something to hold on to, before I can stand from a sitting position or turn around.
27. Don't like crowds or groups of people. Their movements are too unpredictable for me to manoeuvre around them.
28. Can't shop in a superstore because of the crowds and the fact that I cannot train my eyes up and down.
29. When dusting at home, pictures and mirrors are usually left uneven. It may be a few hours before I notice this and can adjust them. However if I go into a hotel or someone's home, I notice straight away if pictures are askew. It makes me feel sick and dizzy looking at them.
30. Can't dance or do any sport except walking.
31. Feel unsure, lack confidence, and avoid situations. Often feel low - less than myself.
32. Movements directly in front of me make me feel disorientated.
33. What I see often looks fragmented, like a smashed mirror effect.
34. No sense of balance in the dark.
35. Often find it difficult to walk in a straight line.

Appendix B

<u>Some useful addresses</u>

I made enquiries at my local hospital and surgery about self-help groups for Benign Paroxysmal Positional Vertigo but there was nothing available locally. I did find information from the societies listed below and the internet. It was comforting to know that I was not alone in my plight and it did allow me to understand my condition.

Brain & Spine Foundation,
7, Winchester House,
Kennington Park,
Cranmer Road,
London.
SW9 6EJ
Tel. O20 7793 5900
www.brainandspine.org.uk/

Booklet called "Dizziness and Balance Problems"

Meniere's Society,
98, Maybury Road,
Woking,
Surrey.
GU1 5HX
Tel. O1483 740597
www.menieres.co.uk/

Information sheets on dizziness and imbalance

RNID,
19-23, Featherstone Street,
London.
EC1Y 8SL
Tel. 0808 808 0123
www.rnid.org.uk

Booklet called "Dizziness and Balance Problems"

__Notes__